LIBERALISM'S POSITIVE IMPACT

ON THE WORLD

LIBERALISM'S POSITIVE IMPACT

ON THE WORLD

LIB CONN & LENNY MARX

PRIMARY PUBS

Primary Pubs

Manufactured in the United States of America

10 9 8 7 6 5 4 3 2 1

Library of Congress

ISBN-13: 978-0-9988451-0-4
ISBN-10:   0-9988451-0-8

For God-fearing, freedom-fighting, pro-life,
anti-big government, rights-preserving patriots

Contents

Chapter 1

Africa

Chapter 2

Antarctica

Chapter 3

Asia

Chapter 4

Australia

Chapter 5

Europe

Chapter 6

North America

Chapter 7

South America

None.

None.

None.

None.

None.

None.

None.

None.

None.

None.

None.

None.

None.

None.

None.

None.

None.

None.

None.

None.

None.

None.

None.

None.

www.ingramcontent.com/pod-product-compliance
Lightning Source LLC
Chambersburg PA
CBHW060635280326
41933CB00012B/2048